DATE DUE		

621.8
WIL

Wilkin, Fred.

Machines.

A New True Book

MACHINES

By Fred Wilkin

CHILDRENS PRESS ®

CHICAGO

Wheel powered by a steam engine

Library of Congress Cataloging-in-Publication Data

Wilkin, Fred.
  Machines.

  (A New true book)
  Includes index.
  Summary: Describes how machines work and the many
kinds of things they can do.
  1. Machinery—Juvenile literature. [1. Machinery]
I. Title.
TJ147.W488 1986   621.8   85-30936
ISBN 0-516-01283-5

TABLE OF CONTENTS

Early hunters (above) and the Aztec people (below) that lived thousands and thousands of years later did all their work without machines.

WITHOUT MACHINES

Once there was a time when people had no machines of any kind.

All work was done by hand or finger or foot. Simple tools were used to poke holes and stitch and cut. Stone hammers pounded on things. Maybe some wooden poles and a rock were used as a lever to help move or push

Water buffalo work in rice paddies in the Phillipines.

something. (A lever is a very simple machine.)

It was natural for the world to be without machines.

Later people added to their own strength by using

Horse-team pulls the type of plow used on farms in the 1800s.

animals. A big ox or a
horse could carry a heavy
load or pull with a
powerful force.

But it took a long, long
time for people to come
up with wheels and other

ways to make things move.
That's what the machines
we know about nowadays
do best.

In a way, it must have
been nice long ago when
nothing was very
complicated. There were
no machines to break
down or wear out. No one
would have to look at a
broken-down machine and
wonder what to do with
it—to fix it or to replace it.

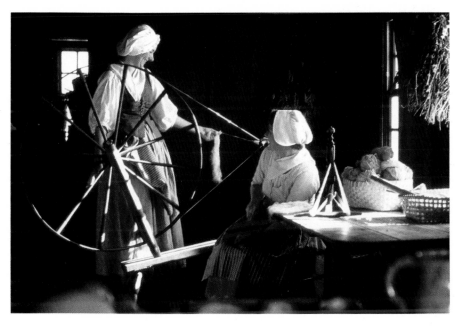

Spinning wheel used by English colonists during the 1600s

HERE COME MACHINES!

Human beings create machines. A machine does not happen by itself all of a sudden out of nothing. It takes a person to figure out what a machine should be. Then somebody builds it.

9

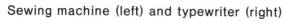
Sewing machine (left) and typewriter (right)

You might have an idea
for a machine some day.
New machines are
invented every day by
someone. It could be you.

In recent times,
machines have become
an important part of our

10

Washer and dryer (left) and lawn mower (right)

lives. This has happened in most parts of the world. In some ways, we could hardly do without machines today. Think of what the machines around you do, and then think of having to do those things by hand.

WHAT MAKES MACHINES GO?

Basically you need a push to make machines go. Or you need lots of constant push and force to get things moving.

There are different ways to tap into energy sources of various kinds. What are they?

Machines require energy. That energy can come from you.

Young girl provides the energy to make her car go.

Energy that makes machines work also can come from other sources like fuels. When fuels are burned, heat energy is given off. Machines use this heat energy to make things move.

Stirling engine in operation

HEAT ENERGY MAKES MACHINES WORK

This toy Stirling engine shows how the heat energy in a flame becomes rotary motion and turns the wheel on the engine.

A Stirling engine works

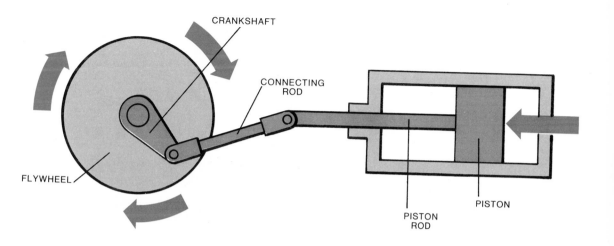

simply because air inside the chamber swells and shrinks rapidly. This causes a piston, hooked to a crankshaft, to move back and forth. The result is round and round motion, which is what most machines provide.

Steam engine belonging to the Rio Grande Railroad (left).
Operating model of a steam-powered tractor (right)

Steam engines use a hot fire and boiling water to produce motion. These engines burn coal, oil, or wood. The heat energy from the fire changes the water inside the boiler into steam.

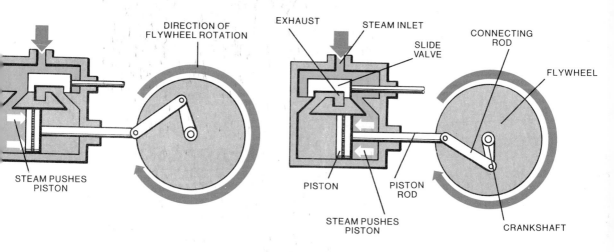

DIRECTION OF FLYWHEEL ROTATION

STEAM PUSHES PISTON

EXHAUST
STEAM INLET
SLIDE VALVE
CONNECTING ROD
FLYWHEEL
PISTON
PISTON ROD
STEAM PUSHES PISTON
CRANKSHAFT

The expanding steam fills up a chamber and pushes on a piston. The steam pushes first on one side of the piston and then on the other causing a back and forth motion.

This back and forth movement of the piston pushes then pulls the

Close-up of the rod, crankshaft, and flywheel. This type of mechanical connection powers many of the world's machines.

connecting rod. The rod, in turn, puts the push on a crankshaft that turns around. A flywheel spins, producing a round and round motion of much spinning force. This kind of connection plays a big part in the machines of the world.

Close-up of a piston and rod

MORE ABOUT PISTONS

Most engines have one or more pistons. Super spinning engines use explosions to push on a piston. That piston moves as a result, forth and back, and back and forth. The piston's power is connected to a crank to produce the round and round motion in the machine. Out comes torque, or a twisting force, and a flywheel keeps it coasting between explosions.

Some engines use a fuel like gasoline or diesel oil that burns in a flash to release heat.

Internal combustion engines power nearly every kind of car and truck. The

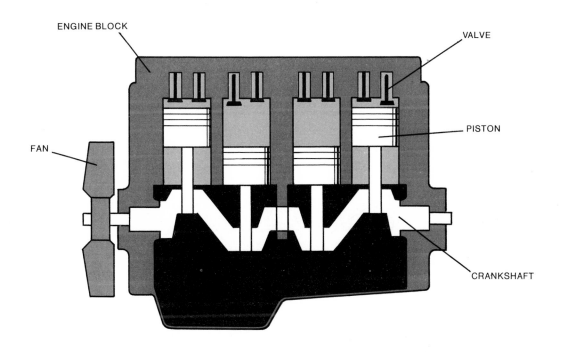

ENGINE BLOCK

VALVE

PISTON

FAN

CRANKSHAFT

machine runs, and the motion of the tire on the pavement moves the vehicle along.

Pushes and pulls have become a steady force to produce motion.

MAKING MACHINES TAKES MACHINERY

Machines have moving parts. No machine would work if it were unmovable. A machine is an action thing.

Machines have many parts that must be made first, and then put together. Some machines can build parts. But those machines must be built, too. And so on. . . .

Many machines are used in this steel fabricating factory.

Machine shops are places where people use machines to cut, shape, hammer, and drill materials that become machines.

23

Here are toy machines in
a layout that demonstrates
the kind of action that
takes place in a machine
shop.

The Stirling engine is
running to power the
machinery. There are
pulleys making other
wheels go around. In a

Water, directed over this water wheel, was used to grind corn at this mill in the Great Smoky Mountains National Park in Tennessee.

shop, belts and chains can transfer the twisting force from a single engine. In past times, a waterwheel was used. But waterwheels and mills needed a steady stream of water. Those places were limited. A mill powered by a heat engine

Paper cups (left) and paper (right) are made by machine.

could operate anywhere,
anytime.

Factories full of all kinds
of machinery were started
up in many places. They
made threads and cloth
and sewing machines.
They cut lumber and made

Inspector checks air in football (left). Robots (right) work without humans on this Ford Motor Company assembly line.

furniture. Cars and trucks were made in factories by machines. Metals were bored and trimmed. Wire was pulled and shaped. There's a long, long list of what factory machinery can make.

Collection of early machines is displayed at the Henry Ford Museum

WHAT DO MACHINES DO?

Machines push. Machines pull. Most of the time machines twist. The round and round motion is what is used most. But a machine might do many

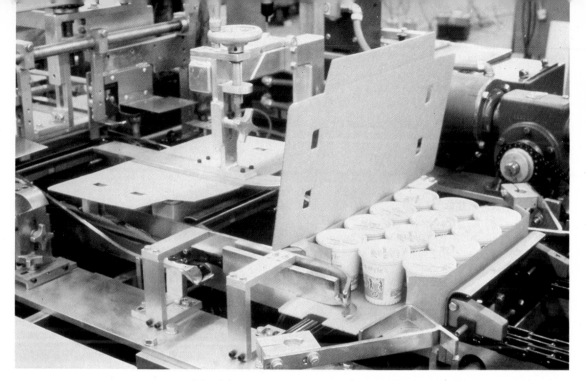

Machines are used to pack products on this assembly line.

things all at once—a
combination of push, pull,
twist, punch, tear, stamp,
rip, slice, squeeze, or
jiggle. A machine will squirt
if it's a pump. You can get
a machine to do just about
anything you want. It

29

Conveyor belts (above)
and huge cranes (right)

depends on how you build
the machine and what it is
intended to do.

Do you want it to lift
materials high for
buildings? Do you want it
to scoop and move coal?
Should it crush rocks into
powder? Or will it be made

Tiny gears in a watch (left) and huge
earth movers (right) are also examples of machines.

to drill tiny holes for tiny
screws?

Collect pictures of the
many kinds of machines
and what they do. You
might want to build models
of machines yourself.

31

HUMANS AND MACHINES

Many people fancy old cars. They fix them up and are proud of them. There is beauty in these machines. Old ones were simple.

Mr. Roorda and a restored Model "T" Ford

Close-up of an automobile engine

Today automobiles have become more complicated. Sometimes it is difficult to know what is under the hood. There are so many bits and pieces that hide the real workings, which are really only simple pistons and cranks.

A MEASURING MACHINE

How thick is the paper used for pages in this book? Or what is the thickness of a thin sheet of brass metal? A micrometer is a machine tool, a twisting screw that

Micrometer

measures very fine
differences in thickness.

It works on a large scale
by adjusting the space
between two bolts on a
threaded screw. A screw is
one of the simple machines.

Flying Falcons (left)
and modern jet (above)

FLYING MACHINES

What are more wonderful
than flying machines? They
are heavier than air, yet
they can climb into the
sky. It takes energy to spin
an airscrew or propeller.

Jet engines are a

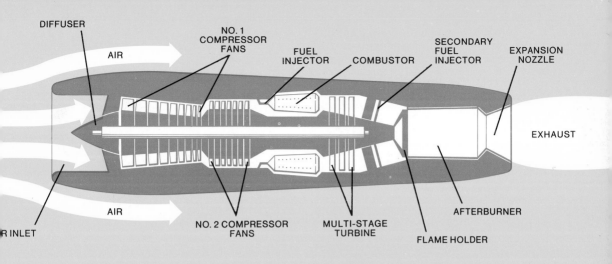

DIFFUSER

AIR

NO. 1 COMPRESSOR FANS

FUEL INJECTOR

COMBUSTOR

SECONDARY FUEL INJECTOR

EXPANSION NOZZLE

EXHAUST

R INLET

AIR

NO. 2 COMPRESSOR FANS

MULTI-STAGE TURBINE

AFTERBURNER

FLAME HOLDER

combination of spinning fans and turbines. Their thrust is from burning fuel in finely-made machinery that rotates at extremely high speed.

Flying machines slice through air, which gives a lifting force.

A SUN MACHINE

Turning the sun's energy into motion is what a sun machine does. However, just about all it can do is spin. There is no way for it to be harnessed to do any useful work.

Air is heated on the dark side more than on the light side of each vane. Tiny bits of the air that remains in the glass bulb bounce off the hotter

Heat from the sun turns the vanes in this machine.

surface. This causes the vanes to turn away from the "kicking air."

This is an energy machine with only a single moving part. It tells you a lot about heated surfaces, air, and motion.

ELECTRICAL MACHINES

Waterwheels, gas or steam engines, or even windmills are machines that turn electrical generators to produce electricity. They each can make electricity flow in wires over long distances by spinning magnets and wires around one another rapidly. That's what a generator is—a machine that converts motion

Traditional windmill (left)
and modern windmills (right)

between magnets and coils
of wire into electrical
current.

On the other hand, an
electrical motor is a form
of machine that converts
the current back into
motion for use in other
machinery.

Electric motor at rest (above)
and in operation (right)

This little demonstration motor spins as the result of pulses of magnetic force that pull the iron part around rapidly. Most machines use spinning motion. Wire and switches deliver the energy to operate the machine.

OLD MACHINES

Looking at old machines
and figuring out what they
did and how they did it
can be interesting. Some
museums have all kinds of
machines that date far
back into history.

Old-time machines are
the most fun to watch. And
the people who designed
and built them must have
enjoyed putting them

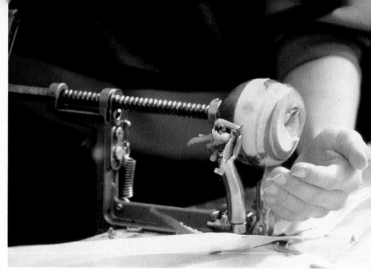

Hand-powered butter churn (left)
and apple peeler (above)

together. Their idea was to
simply make something
work. Often the working
parts were in plain view.
Parts were decorated and
painted and shaped to be
attractive. Anyone could
see the machine's
swishing, clanking,

Carnival ride at a county fair

swinging, and turning parts.

Machines are beautiful
things not only for how
they look but also for what
they do. Machines are built
to do work better or
quicker or cheaper.
Machines make life easier
for all of us.

WORDS YOU SHOULD KNOW

airscrew(AIR • skroo) — a propeller for an airplane

energy(EN • er • jee) — the ability or power to do work

flywheel(FLY • weel) — a heavy, turning wheel that helps to keep constant the speed of a machine

generator(JEN • uh • rate • er) — a machine that converts mechanical energy into electrical energy

lever(LEHV • er) — a straight strong bar or rod used to exert pressure

micrometer(my • KROM • ut • er) — a machine tool that measures precise thicknesses

piston(PIS • tun) — a sliding piece of machinery, connected to a crank that produces motion in a machine

pulley(PULL • lee) — a wheel that is turned by means of a rope or belt in order to move something

rotary(ROWT • uh • ree) — turning in a circular motion, like a wheel on an axle

screw(SKROO) — a simple machine with spiral threads, used for turning or fastening

steam(STEEM) — hot vapor from boiling water, used to move pistons in machines

torque(TORK) — a force that produces rotation or a twisting motion

turbine(TER • bun) — A rotary engine, usually powered by water or steam, that has a series of curved blades that rotate

waterwheel(WAWT • er • weel) — a wheel that is made to turn by the force of moving water

INDEX

About the author

Fred Wilkin, Jr. is the Chairman of Natural Science at National College of Education. He has written scripts and acted as science consultant for a number of films and film strips on natural phenomena for Journal Films *and* SVE. *Dr. Wilkin also has written science investigations for Ginn's science programs for grades 1 through 8.*